WHAT'S COOKING?

PASTA

PARRAGON

First published in Great Britain in 1997 by
Parragon
Unit 13–17
Avonbridge Trading Estate
Atlantic Road
Avonmouth
Bristol BS11 9QD

ISBN: 0-7525-2257-4

Produced by Haldane Mason, London

Acknowledgements
Art Director: Ron Samuels
Editors: Jo-Anne Cox, Charles Dixon-Spain
Design: Zoë Mellors
Photography: Amanda Heywood

Printed in Italy

Material in this book has previously appeared in
Pasta by Pamela Westland, *Quick & Easy Meals*
by Carole Handslip and *Cooking on a Budget* by
Sue Ashworth.

Note
Cup measurements in this book are for
American cups. Tablespoons are assumed to be
15 ml. Unless otherwise stated, milk is assumed
to be full-fat, eggs are standard size 3 and
pepper is freshly ground black pepper.

CONTENTS

Introduction 4

Introduction

Pasta is a universal favourite – easy to cook, economical and marvellously versatile. This excellent collection of recipes has something for everyone, from hearty bakes for family meals to elegant seafood dishes for entertaining.

Pasta means 'paste' or 'dough' in Italian, and many of the widely popular pasta dishes have their origins in Italy, where pasta has been produced at least as far back as the 13th century. Its principal ingredient, durum wheat, is modest enough, but more and more types of fresh and dried pasta are coming on to the market to inspire new variations on tried and tested recipes. As well as green pasta made with spinach, and red pasta flavoured with tomato paste, there are other more unusual colours available: saffron pasta is an attractive orange-yellow colour, beetroot pasta is a deep pink, and pasta coloured with squid ink is a dramatic black. You can also buy or make pasta flecked with chopped basil and other herbs.

The enjoyment of pasta depends on its being cooked to perfection; not too little, when it will be crisp and unyielding and taste of raw flour, and not too much, when it will be too soft and the strands or shapes will probably stick together. Instructions for cooking perfect pasta are given on page 59.

Available in a wide variety of shapes, the versatility of pasta makes it suitable for a wide variety of dishes. The recipes in this book begin with appetizers, salads and light meals, then delicious seafood dishes are followed by classic meat dishes such as Spaghetti Carbonara and Lasagne. Pasta is also ideally suited to vegetarian dishes, with a selection here ranging from a warming winter casserole to a tasty stir-fry.

Vegetable & Pasta Salad

This is delicious served with cold meats.

SERVES 4

2 small aubergines (eggplant), thinly sliced
1 large onion, sliced
2 large beef-steak tomatoes, skinned and cut into wedges
1 red (bell) pepper, cored, deseeded and sliced
1 fennel bulb, thinly sliced • 2 garlic cloves, sliced
4 tbsp olive oil
175 g/6 oz small pasta shapes, such as bows
90 g/3 oz/½ cup Feta cheese, crumbled
a few basil leaves, torn • salt and pepper
salad leaves (greens), to serve

Dressing:

5 tbsp olive oil • juice of 1 orange
1 tsp grated orange zest • ¼ tsp paprika
4 canned anchovies, finely chopped • pepper

1 Place the aubergines (eggplant) in a colander, sprinkle with salt and set aside for about 1 hour to draw out the juices. Rinse under cold, running water to remove the salt, then dry on paper towels.

2 Arrange the aubergines (eggplant), onion, tomatoes, (bell) pepper, fennel and garlic in a single layer in an ovenproof dish, sprinkle on 3 tablespoons of the olive oil and season. Bake uncovered in a preheated oven, 220°C/425°F/Gas Mark 7, for 45 minutes or until the vegetables begin to turn brown. Remove from the oven and set aside to cool.

3 Cook the pasta (see page 59). Transfer the drained pasta to a bowl.

4 To make the dressing, mix together the oil, orange juice and zest and paprika. Stir in the anchovies

and season with pepper. Pour the dressing over the pasta while it is hot, and toss well. Set the pasta aside to cool.

5 To assemble the salad, line a shallow serving dish with the salad leaves (greens), spoon the pasta in a layer over the leaves, and arrange the cold roasted vegetables in the centre. Scatter over the Feta cheese and basil leaves. Serve at once.

Spicy Sausage Salad

A warm sausage and pasta dressing spooned over chilled salad leaves makes a refreshing combination with which to start a meal.

SERVES 4

125g/ 4 oz small pasta shapes, such as elbow tubetti
3 tbsp olive oil
1 medium onion, chopped
2 cloves garlic, crushed
1 small yellow (bell) pepper, cored,
seeded and cut into matchstick strips
175 g/ 6 oz spicy pork sausage such as chorizo,
skinned and sliced
2 tbsp red wine
1 tbsp red wine vinegar
mixed salad leaves, chilled
salt

1 Cook the pasta as described on page 59. Set aside the drained pasta.

2 Heat 2 tablespoons of the oil in a saucepan over a medium heat. Fry the onion until it is translucent, stir in the garlic, (bell) pepper and sliced sausage and cook for 3–4 minutes, stirring occasionally.

3 Add the wine, wine vinegar and reserved pasta to the pan, stir to blend well and bring the mixture just to the boil.

4 Arrange the chilled salad leaves on 4 individual serving plates and spoon on the warm sausage and pasta mixture. Serve at once.

Chilled Noodles & (Bell) Pepper Sauce

This is a convenient dish to serve when you are arriving home just before family or friends. You can have it all prepared and ready to assemble in minutes.

SERVES 4–6

250 g/8 oz ribbon noodles, or Chinese egg noodles
1 tbsp sesame oil • 1 red (bell) pepper
1 yellow (bell) pepper • 1 green (bell) pepper
6 spring onions (scallions), cut into matchsticks • salt

Dressing:

5 tbsp sesame oil • 2 tbsp light soy sauce
1 tbsp tahini (sesame paste) • 4–5 drops hot pepper sauce

1 Preheat the grill (broiler) to medium. Cook the noodles in a large pan of boiling, salted water until they are almost tender. Drain in a colander, run cold water over them and drain again thoroughly. Tip the noodles into a bowl, stir in the sesame oil, cover and chill.

2 Cook the (bell) peppers under the grill (broiler), turning them frequently, until they are blackened on all sides. Plunge them into cold water, then skin them. Cut in half, remove the core and seeds and cut the flesh into thick strips. Set aside, covered.

3 To make the dressing, mix together the sesame oil, soy sauce, tahini (sesame paste) and hot pepper sauce.

4 Pour the dressing over the noodles, reserving 1 tablespoon, and toss well. Turn the noodles into a serving dish, arrange the (bell) pepper strips over the noodles and spoon on the reserved dressing. Scatter over the spring onion (scallion) strips.

Spaghetti with Ricotta Cheese Sauce

This makes a quick and easy starter, ideal for the summer months.

SERVES 4

350 g/ 12 oz spaghetti • 1 tbsp olive oil
45 g/ 1½ oz/ 3 tbsp butter, cut into small pieces
2 tbsp chopped parsley

Sauce:
125 g/ 4 oz/ 1 cup freshly ground almonds
125 g/ 4 oz/ ½ cup Ricotta
large pinch of grated nutmeg
large pinch of ground cinnamon
150 ml/ ¼ pint/ ⅔ cup crème fraîche
2 tbsp olive oil
120 ml/ 4 fl oz/ ½ cup hot chicken stock
1 tbsp pine kernels
freshly ground black pepper
coriander leaves, to garnish

1 Cook the pasta as described on page 59. Return the drained pasta to the pan and toss with the butter and parsley. Cover the pan and keep warm.

2 To make the sauce, mix together the ground almonds, Ricotta, nutmeg, cinnamon and crème fraîche to make a thick paste. Gradually pour on the oil, stirring constantly until it is well blended. Gradually pour on the hot stock, stirring all the time, until the sauce is smooth.

3 Transfer the spaghetti to a warmed serving dish, pour on the sauce and toss well. Sprinkle each serving with pine kernels and garnish with coriander leaves. Serve warm.

Chicken Scallops

**Served in scallop shells, this dish makes
a stylish presentation for a dinner-party
first course.**

SERVES 4

175 g/ 6 oz short-cut macaroni, or other short pasta shapes
3 tbsp vegetable oil, plus extra for brushing
1 medium onion, finely chopped
3 rashers unsmoked collar or back bacon,
rind removed, chopped
125 g/ 4 oz button mushrooms, thinly sliced or chopped
175 g/ 6 oz cooked chicken, diced
175 ml/ 6 fl oz/ ³⁄4 cup crème fraîche
4 tbsp dry breadcrumbs
60 g/ 2 oz/ ³⁄4 cup mature (sharp) Cheddar cheese, grated
salt and pepper
flat-leaved parsley sprigs, to garnish

1 Cook the pasta as described on page 59. Return the drained pasta to the pan and cover.

2 Heat the grill (broiler) to medium. Heat the remaining oil in a pan over a medium heat and fry the onion until it is translucent. Add the chopped bacon and mushrooms and cook for 3–4 minutes, stirring occasionally. Stir in the pasta, chicken and crème fraîche and season with salt and pepper.

3 Brush 4 large scallop shells with oil. Spoon in the chicken mixture and smooth to make neat mounds.

4 Mix together the breadcrumbs and cheese and sprinkle over the top of the shells. Press the topping lightly into the chicken mixture, and grill (broil) for 4–5 minutes, until golden brown and bubbling. Garnish with parsley sprigs, and serve hot.

Spaghetti with Seafood

Frozen shelled prawns (shrimp) can be used in this colourful and tasty dish.

SERVES 4

*250 g/8 oz short-cut spaghetti, or long spaghetti broken into
15 cm/6 inch lengths
2 tbsp olive oil • 300 ml/½ pint/1¼ cups chicken stock
1 tsp lemon juice • 1 small cauliflower, cut into florets
2 carrots, sliced thinly
125 g/4 oz mangetout (snow peas), trimmed
60 g/2 oz/4 tbsp butter • 1 onion, sliced
250 g/8 oz courgettes (zucchini), sliced thinly
1 garlic clove, chopped
350 g/12 oz frozen shelled prawns (shrimp), defrosted
2 tbsp chopped fresh parsley
30 g/1 oz/¼ cup Parmesan, grated
½ tsp paprika • salt and pepper
4 unshelled prawns (shrimp), to garnish (optional)*

1 Cook the pasta as described on page 59. Return the drained pasta to the pan and stir in the remaining olive oil. Cover and keep warm.

2 Bring the chicken stock and lemon juice to the boil. Add the cauliflower and carrots and cook for 3–4 minutes until they are just tender. Remove with a slotted spoon and set aside. Add the mangetout (snow peas) and cook for 1–2 minutes, until they begin to soften. Remove with a slotted spoon and add to the carrots. Reserve the stock for future use.

3 Melt half the butter in a frying pan (skillet) over a medium heat and fry the onion and courgettes (zucchini) for about 3 minutes. Add the garlic and prawns (shrimp) and cook for 2–3 minutes until thoroughly heated through. Stir in the reserved vegetables and heat through. Season with salt

and pepper then stir in the remaining butter.

4 Transfer the spaghetti to a warmed serving dish. Pour on the sauce and parsley. Toss well using 2 forks, until thoroughly coated. Sprinkle on the grated cheese and paprika, and garnish with unshelled prawns (shrimp), if using. Serve immediately.

Macaroni & Prawn (Shrimp) Bake

This adaptation of an 18th-century Italian dish is served cut into wedges, like a cake.

SERVES 4

350 g/12 oz short pasta, such as short-cut macaroni
1 tbsp olive oil, plus extra for brushing
90 g/3 oz/6 tbsp butter, plus extra for greasing
2 small fennel bulbs, sliced thinly, leaves reserved
175 g/6 oz mushrooms, sliced thinly
175 g/6 oz shelled prawns (shrimp)
Béchamel Sauce (page 58) • *pinch of cayenne pepper*
60 g/2 oz/¾ cup Parmesan, grated • *2 tomatoes, sliced*
1 tsp dried oregano • *salt and pepper*

1 Cook the pasta as described on page 59. Return the drained pasta to the saucepan and dot with 30 g/1 oz/2 tablespoons of the butter. Shake the pan well, cover and keep warm.

2 Melt the remaining butter in a pan over a medium heat and fry the fennel for 3–4 minutes, until it begins to soften. Stir in the mushrooms and fry for a further 2 minutes. Stir in the prawns (shrimp), remove the pan from the heat and set aside, covered.

3 Make the béchamel sauce and add the cayenne pepper. Remove the pan from the heat and stir in the reserved vegetables, prawns (shrimp) and the pasta. Grease a round, shallow baking dish. Pour in the pasta mixture and spread evenly. Sprinkle on the Parmesan, and arrange the tomato slices in a ring on top. Brush the tomato with oil and sprinkle on the dried oregano.

4 Bake in a preheated oven, 180°C/350°F/Gas Mark 4, for 25 minutes, until golden brown. Serve hot.

Seafood Lasagne

A delicious variation of a classic pasta dish.

SERVES 6

8 sheets wholewheat lasagne • 1 tbsp olive oil
500 g/1 lb smoked cod • 600 ml/1 pint/2½ cups milk
1 tbsp lemon juice • 8 peppercorns
2 bay leaves • a few parsley stalks
60 g/2 oz/¾ cup mature (sharp) Cheddar, grated
30 g/1 oz/½ cup Parmesan, grated
a few whole prawns (shrimp), to garnish (optional)

Sauce:

60 g/2 oz/¼ cup butter, plus extra for greasing
1 large onion, sliced
1 green (bell) pepper, cored, deseeded and chopped
1 small courgette (zucchini), sliced • 60 g/2 oz/½ cup flour
150 ml/¼ pint/⅔ cup white wine
150 ml/¼ pint/⅔ cup single (light) cream
125 g/4 oz shelled prawns (shrimp)
60 g/2 oz/½ cup mature (sharp) Cheddar, grated
salt and pepper

1 Cook the lasagne as described on page 36.

2 Place the cod, milk, lemon juice, peppercorns, bay leaves and parsley stalks in a frying pan (skillet). Bring to the boil, cover and simmer for 10 minutes. Lift the fish out with a slotted spoon. Remove the skin and bones and flake the fish with a fork. Strain and reserve the liquor.

3 Make the sauce: melt the butter in a pan and cook the onion, (bell) pepper and courgette (zucchini) for 2–3 minutes. Stir in the flour and cook for 1 minute. Stir in the fish liquor, wine, cream and prawns (shrimp), and simmer for 2 minutes. Remove from heat, add cheese, and season.

4 Grease a shallow baking dish. Pour in a quarter of

the sauce and spread evenly over the base. Cover the sauce with 3 sheets of lasagne, then with another quarter of the sauce. Arrange the fish on top, then cover with half the remaining sauce. Finish with the remaining lasagne, then the rest of the sauce. Sprinkle the Cheddar and Parmesan over the sauce.

5 Bake in a preheated oven, 190°C/375°F/ Gas Mark 5, for 25 minutes, or until the top is golden brown and bubbling. Garnish with a few whole prawns (shrimp), if liked.

Pasta Shells with Mussels

An aromatic and garlicky seafood dish.

SERVES 4–6

425 g/14 oz pasta shells • 1 tbsp olive oil

Sauce:
3.5 litres/6 pints mussels, scrubbed
250 ml/8 fl oz/1 cup dry white wine
2 large onions, chopped
125 g/4 oz/½ cup unsalted butter
6 large garlic cloves, chopped finely
5 tbsp chopped fresh parsley
300 ml/½ pint/1¼ cups double (heavy) cream
salt and pepper • crusty bread, to serve

1 Pull off the 'beards' from the mussels and rinse well in several changes of water. Discard any that do not close when tapped. Put the mussels in a large pan with the white wine and half the onions. Cover the pan, shake and cook over a medium heat for 2–3 minutes until the mussels open. Remove from the heat, lift out the mussels with a slotted spoon, reserving the liquor, and set aside until they are cool enough to handle. Discard any mussels that have not opened.

2 Melt the butter in a pan over a medium heat and fry the remaining onion until translucent. Stir in the garlic and cook for 1 minute. Gradually pour on the reserved cooking liquor, stirring to blend well. Stir in the parsley and cream. Season and bring to simmering point.

3 Cook the pasta as described on page 59. Return the pasta to the pan, cover and keep warm.

4 Remove the mussels from their shells, reserving a few shells for garnish. Stir the mussels into the cream sauce. Tip the pasta into a warmed serving dish, pour on the

sauce and mix. Garnish
with a few mussel shells
and serve hot, with warm,
crusty bread.

Spaghetti with Smoked Salmon

Made in moments, this is a dish to impress and delight unexpected guests.

SERVES 4

500 g/ 1 lb buckwheat spaghetti
2 tbsp olive oil
90 g/ 3 oz/ ½ cup Feta cheese, crumbled
coriander (cilantro) or parsley, to garnish

Sauce:
300 ml/ ½ pint/ 1¼ cups double (heavy) cream
150 ml/ ¼ pint/ ⅔ cup whisky or brandy
125 g/ 4 oz smoked salmon
large pinch of cayenne pepper
2 tbsp chopped fresh coriander (cilantro) or parsley
salt and pepper

1 Cook the pasta as described on page 59. Return the drained pasta to the pan and sprinkle on the remaining oil. Cover and shake the pan, then set aside and keep warm.

2 In separate small pans, heat the cream and the whisky or brandy to simmering point. Do not let them boil.

3 Combine the cream with the whisky or brandy. Cut the smoked salmon into thin strips and add to the cream mixture. Season with pepper and cayenne, and stir in the coriander (cilantro) or parsley.

4 Transfer the spaghetti to a warmed serving dish, pour on the sauce and toss thoroughly using 2 large forks. Scatter the Feta cheese over the pasta and garnish with the coriander (cilantro) or parsley. Serve hot.

Vermicelli with Clam Sauce

A quickly cooked seafood dish with style.

SERVES 4

425 g/14 oz vermicelli, spaghetti, or other long pasta
1 tbsp olive oil • 30 g/1 oz/2 tbsp butter
2 tbsp Parmesan shavings, to garnish
sprig of basil, to garnish

Sauce:
1 tbsp olive oil • 2 onions, chopped
2 garlic cloves, chopped
2 × 200 g/7 oz jars of clams in brine
120 ml/4 fl oz/½ cup white wine
4 tbsp chopped fresh parsley • ½ tsp dried oregano
pinch of freshly grated nutmeg • salt and pepper

1 Cook the pasta as described on page 59. Return the drained pasta to the pan and add the butter. Cover and shake the pan, then set aside and keep warm.

2 To make the clam sauce, heat the oil in a pan over a medium heat and fry the onion until it is translucent. Stir in the garlic and cook for 1 minute. Strain the brine from 1 jar of clams, pour into the pan and add the wine. Stir well and simmer for 3 minutes. Drain the brine from the second jar of clams and discard.

3 Add the clams and herbs to the pan, and season with pepper and nutmeg. Lower the heat and cook until the sauce is heated through.

4 Transfer the pasta to a warmed serving dish and pour over the sauce. Sprinkle with the Parmesan shavings and garnish with the sprig of basil. Serve hot.

Spaghetti with Tuna & Parsley Sauce

This is a recipe to look forward to when parsley is at its most prolific, during the summer.

SERVES 4

500 g / 1 lb spaghetti
1 tbsp olive oil
30 g / 1 oz / 2 tbsp butter
black olives, to garnish

Sauce:

200 g / 7 oz can of tuna, drained
60 g / 2 oz can of anchovies, drained
250 ml / 8 fl oz / 1 cup olive oil
60 g / 2 oz / 1 cup roughly chopped fresh, flat-leaf parsley
150 ml / ¼ pint / ⅔ cup crème fraîche
salt and pepper

1 Cook the spaghetti as described on page 59. Return the drained pasta to the pan, add the butter, toss thoroughly to coat, cover and keep warm.

2 To make the sauce, remove any bones from the tuna. Put it into a blender or food processor with the anchovies, olive oil and parsley and process until the sauce is smooth. Pour in the crème fraîche and process for a few seconds to blend. Taste the sauce and season.

3 Warm 4 plates. Warm the pan of spaghetti over a medium heat, shaking, until it is heated through. Pour on the sauce and toss quickly, using 2 forks.

4 Transfer to the serving plates, garnish with the olives and serve hot.

Steamed Pasta Pudding

A tasty mixture of creamy fish and macaroni cooked in a bowl.

SERVES 4

125 g/4 oz short-cut macaroni, or other short pasta shapes
1 tbsp olive oil
15 g/½ oz/1 tbsp butter, plus extra for greasing
500 g/1 lb white fish fillets, such as cod, haddock or coley
a few parsley stalks • 6 black peppercorns
120 ml/4 fl oz/½ cup double (heavy) cream
2 eggs, separated • 2 tbsp chopped fresh dill, or parsley
freshly ground black pepper • freshly grated nutmeg
60 g/2 oz/¾ cup Parmesan, grated
Tomato Sauce (page 58), to serve
dill or parsley sprigs, to garnish

1 Cook the pasta as described on page 59. Return the drained pasta to the pan, add the butter and cover the pan. Keep warm.

2 Place the fish in a frying pan (skillet) with the parsley stalks, peppercorns and just enough water to cover. Bring to the boil, cover, and simmer for 10 minutes. Lift out the fish with a fish slice, reserving the liquor. When the fish is cool enough to handle, skin and remove any remaining bones. Cut into bite-sized pieces.

3 Transfer the pasta to a large bowl and stir in the cream, egg yolks, dill and pepper. Stir in the fish and enough liquor to make the mixture moist but firm; it should fall easily from a spoon but not be too runny. Whisk the egg whites until stiff, then fold into the mixture.

4 Grease a heatproof bowl or pudding basin and spoon in the mixture to within 4 cm/1½ inches of the rim. Cover the top with greased baking parchment and a cloth, or with foil, and tie firmly around the rim.

5 Stand the pudding on a trivet in a large pan of boiling water to come halfway up the sides. Cover and steam for 1½ hours, topping up the boiling water as needed.

6 Run a knife around the inside of the bowl and invert on to a warmed serving dish. Pour tomato sauce over the top and garnish with the herb sprigs. Serve the nutmeg and Parmesan separately.

Squid & Macaroni Stew

This seafood dish is quick and easy to make, yet is deliciously satisfying to eat.

SERVES 4–6

250 g/ 8 oz short-cut macaroni, or other short pasta shapes
1 tbsp olive oil • 2 tbsp chopped fresh parsley
salt and pepper • crusty bread, to serve

Sauce:

6 tbsp olive oil • 2 onions, sliced
350 g/ 12 oz cleaned squid, cut into 4 cm/½ inch strips
250 ml/ 8 fl oz/ 1 cup fish stock
150 ml/ ¼ pint/ ⅔ cup red wine
350 g/ 12 oz tomatoes, peeled and thinly sliced
2 tbsp tomato purée (paste) • 1 tsp dried oregano
2 bay leaves • salt and pepper

1 Cook the pasta for only 3 minutes in a pan of boiling salted water, adding the oil. Drain, return to the pan, cover and keep warm.

2 To make the sauce, heat the oil in a pan over medium heat and fry the onion until translucent. Add the squid and stock and simmer for 5 minutes. Pour on the wine and add the tomatoes, tomato purée (paste), oregano and bay leaves. Bring to the boil, season and cook, uncovered, for 5 minutes.

3 Add the pasta, stir well, cover the pan and simmer for 10 minutes, or until the squid and pasta are almost tender. The sauce should be syrupy; if it is too liquid, continue cooking, uncovered, for a few minutes. Adjust the seasoning if necessary.

4 Remove the bay leaves and stir in most of the parsley, reserving a little to garnish. Transfer to a warmed serving dish. Sprinkle on the remaining parsley and serve hot with warm, crusty bread such as ciabatta.

Spaghetti Bolognese

This familiar meat sauce, known as ragù, may also be used in lasagne.

SERVES 4

425 g/14 oz spaghetti • 1 tbsp olive oil • salt
15 g/½ oz/1 tbsp butter
2 tbsp chopped fresh parsley, to garnish

Ragù:

3 tbsp olive oil • 45 g/1½ oz/3 tbsp butter
2 large onions, chopped • 4 celery stalks, sliced thinly
175 g/6 oz streaky bacon, chopped into small strips
2 garlic cloves, chopped
500 g/1 lb minced (ground) lean beef
2 tbsp tomato purée (paste) • 1 tbsp flour
425 g/14 oz can of chopped tomatoes
150 ml/¼ pint/⅔ cup beef stock
150 ml/¼ pint/⅔ cup red wine • 2 tsp dried oregano
½ tsp freshly grated nutmeg • salt and pepper

1 To make the ragù: heat the oil and the butter in a large frying pan (skillet) over a medium heat. Add the onions, celery and bacon pieces and fry for 5 minutes, stirring occasionally.

2 Stir in the garlic and minced (ground) beef and cook, stirring, until the meat has lost its redness. Lower the heat and continue cooking for a further 10 minutes, stirring occasionally.

3 Increase the heat to medium, stir in the tomato purée (paste) and the flour and cook for 1–2 minutes. Stir in the chopped tomatoes, beef stock and wine, and bring to the boil, stirring. Season with salt and pepper and stir in the oregano and nutmeg. Cover the pan and simmer for 45 minutes, stirring occasionally.

4 Cook the spaghetti as described on page 59.

Return the drained pasta to the pan. Dot the spaghetti with the butter and toss thoroughly.

5 Pour the sauce over the spaghetti and toss well. Garnish with the parsley and serve immediately.

Lasagne Verde

The sauce in this delicious baked pasta dish is the same sauce that is served with Spaghetti Bolognese (page 34).

SERVES 6

Ragù (page 34) • *1 tbsp olive oil*
250 g/8 oz lasagne verde
60 g/2 oz/³/₄ cup Parmesan, grated
Béchamel Sauce (page 58) • *salt and pepper*
green salad, tomato salad or black olives, to serve

1 Begin by making the ragù as described on page 34. Cook for 10–12 minutes longer than the time given in an uncovered pan to reduce the sauce to the consistency of a thick paste.

2 Have ready a large pan of boiling, salted water and add the olive oil. Drop the pasta sheets into the boiling water a few at a time, and return the water to the boil before adding more pasta sheets. If you are using fresh lasagne, cook the sheets for 8 minutes. Cook dried or partly precooked pasta according to the directions on the packet. Remove the pasta sheets from the pan with a slotted spoon. Spread them in a single layer on damp tea towels.

3 Grease a rectangular ovenproof dish, about 25–28 cm/10–11 inches long. To assemble the lasagne verde, spoon a little of the ragù into the prepared dish, cover with a layer of lasagne, then spoon over a little béchamel sauce and sprinkle over some of the cheese. Continue making layers in this way, covering the final layer of lasagne with the remaining béchamel sauce.

4 Sprinkle on the remaining cheese and bake in a preheated oven, 190°C/ 375°F/Gas Mark 5, for 40 minutes, until the sauce is golden brown and bubbling. Serve with a green salad, a tomato salad, or a bowl of black olives.

Pasticcio

A recipe with both Italian and Greek origins, this dish may be served hot or cold.

SERVES 6

250 g/ 8 oz fusilli, or other short pasta shapes
1 tbsp olive oil • 4 tbsp double (heavy) cream
salt • sprigs of rosemary to garnish

Sauce:

2 tbsp olive oil, plus extra for brushing • 1 onion, sliced thinly
1 red (bell) pepper, cored, deseeded and chopped
2 garlic cloves, chopped
625 g/ 1¼ lb minced (ground) lean beef
425 g/ 14 oz can of chopped tomatoes
120 ml/ 4 fl oz/ ½ cup dry white wine
2 tbsp chopped fresh parsley
60 g/ 2 oz can of anchovies, drained and chopped
salt and pepper

Topping:

300 ml/ ½ pint/ 1¼ cups natural yogurt • 3 eggs
pinch of freshly grated nutmeg
45 g/ 1½ oz/ ½ cup Parmesan, grated • salt and pepper

1 To make the sauce, heat the oil in a large frying pan (skillet) and fry the onion and (bell) pepper for 3 minutes. Stir in the garlic and cook for 1 minute. Stir in the beef and cook, stirring frequently, until it is no longer pink. Add the tomatoes and wine, stir well and bring to the boil. Simmer, uncovered, for 20 minutes, until the sauce is fairly thick. Stir in the parsley and anchovies, and season to taste.

2 Cook the pasta as described on page 59. Transfer the drained pasta to a bowl. Stir in the cream and set aside.

3 To make the topping, beat together the yogurt and eggs and season with nutmeg, and salt and pepper. Stir in the cheese.

4 Brush a shallow baking dish with oil. Spoon in half the pasta and cover with half the meat sauce. Repeat these layers, spread the topping evenly and sprinkle on the cheese. Bake in a preheated oven, 190°C/375°F/Gas Mark 5, for 25 minutes, until the topping is golden brown and bubbling. Garnish with rosemary sprigs and serve with a selection of vegetable crudités.

Tagliatelle with Meatballs

There is an appetizing contrast of textures and flavours in this satisfying family dish.

SERVES 4

500 g/ 1 lb minced (ground) lean beef
60 g/ 2 oz/ 1 cup soft white breadcrumbs
1 garlic clove, crushed • 2 tbsp chopped fresh parsley
1 tsp dried oregano • large pinch of freshly grated nutmeg
¼ tsp ground coriander
60 g/ 2 oz/³⁄₄ cup Parmesan, grated • 2–3 tbsp milk
flour, for dusting • 5 tbsp olive oil
425 g/ 14 oz tagliatelli • 30 g/ 1 oz/ 2 tbsp butter, diced
salt • mixed salad, to serve

Sauce:
3 tbsp olive oil • 2 large onions, sliced
2 celery stalks, sliced thinly • 2 garlic cloves, chopped
425 g/ 14 oz can of chopped tomatoes
125 g/ 4 oz bottled sun-dried tomatoes, drained and chopped
2 tbsp tomato purée (paste) • 1 tbsp dark muscovado sugar
150 ml/ ¼ pint/²⁄₃ cup white wine, or water
salt and pepper

1 To make the sauce, heat the oil in a pan and fry the onion and celery until translucent. Add the garlic and cook for 1 minute. Stir in the tomatoes, tomato purée (paste), sugar and wine, and season. Bring to the boil and simmer for 10 minutes.

2 Break up the meat in a bowl with a wooden spoon until it becomes a sticky paste. Stir in the breadcrumbs, garlic, herbs and spices. Stir in the cheese and enough milk to make a firm paste. Flour your hands, take large spoonfuls of the mixture and shape it into 12 balls. Heat 4 tablespoons of the oil in a frying pan (skillet) and fry the meatballs for 5–6 minutes until browned.

3 Pour the tomato sauce over the meatballs. Lower the heat, cover the pan and simmer for 30 minutes, turning occasionally. Add a little extra water if the sauce begins to dry out.

4 Cook the pasta as described on page 59. Turn into a warmed serving dish, dot with the butter and toss with two forks. Spoon the meatballs and sauce over the pasta and sprinkle on the parsley. Serve with a mixed salad.

Stuffed Cannelloni

Cannelloni make perfect containers for close-textured sauces of all kinds.

SERVES 4

8 cannelloni tubes • 1 tbsp olive oil
30 g/1 oz /½ cup Parmesan, grated
fresh herb sprigs, to garnish

Filling:

30 g/1 oz/2 tbsp butter
300 g/10 oz frozen spinach, defrosted and chopped
125 g/4 oz /¾ cup Ricotta
30 g/1 oz/½ cup Parmesan, grated
60 g/2 oz/¼ cup chopped ham
¼ tsp freshly grated nutmeg • 2 tbsp double (heavy) cream
2 eggs, lightly beaten • salt and pepper

Sauce:

30 g/1 oz/2 tbsp butter • 30 g/1 oz/¼ cup flour
300 ml/½ pint/1¼ cups milk • 2 bay leaves
large pinch of grated nutmeg • salt and pepper

1 To make the filling, melt the butter in a pan and stir in the spinach. Stir for 2–3 minutes, then remove the pan from the heat. Stir in the cheeses and the ham. Season with nutmeg, and salt and pepper. Beat in the cream and eggs to make a thick paste. Set aside to cool.

2 Cook the cannelloni in a large pan of boiling salted water, adding the olive oil. When almost tender, after 10–12 minutes, drain and set aside to cool.

3 To make the sauce, melt the butter in a pan, stir in the flour and, when it has formed a *roux*, gradually pour on the milk, stirring all the time. Add the bay leaves, bring to simmering point, and cook for 5 minutes. Season

with nutmeg, salt and pepper. Remove from the heat and discard the bay leaves.

4 Spoon the filling into a piping bag and pipe it into each of the cannelloni tubes. Spoon a little of the sauce into a shallow baking dish. Arrange the cannelloni in a single layer, then pour over the remaining sauce. Sprinkle with Parmesan cheese and bake in a preheated oven, 190°C/ 375°F/Gas Mark 5, for 40–45 minutes, until the sauce is golden brown and bubbling. Serve garnished with fresh herb sprigs.

Spaghetti Carbonara

Ensure that all the cooked ingredients are as hot as possible, so that the beaten eggs are cooked on contact.

SERVES 4

425 g/14 oz spaghetti • 2 tbsp olive oil
1 large onion, sliced thinly • 2 garlic cloves, chopped
175 g/6 oz streaky bacon rashers, rind
removed, cut into thin strips
30 g/1 oz/2 tbsp butter
175 g/6 oz mushrooms, sliced thinly
300 ml/½ pint/1¼ cups double (heavy) cream
3 eggs, beaten
90 g/3 oz/1 cup Parmesan, grated,
plus extra to serve (optional)
salt and pepper • sprigs of sage, to garnish

1 Cook the spaghetti as described on page 59. Return the drained spaghetti to the pan, cover and keep warm.

2 Heat the remaining oil in a frying pan (skillet) over a medium heat. Fry the onion until it is translucent, then add the garlic and bacon and fry until the bacon is crisp. Remove the onion, garlic and bacon with a slotted spoon and set aside to keep warm. Heat the butter in the pan, add the mushrooms and fry for 3–4 minutes, stirring occasionally. Return the bacon mixture to the pan with the mushrooms. Cover and keep warm.

3 Mix the cream, beaten eggs and cheese in a bowl, and season with salt and pepper.

4 Working quickly, tip the spaghetti into the bacon and mushroom mixture and pour on the eggs. Toss the spaghetti quickly, using 2 forks, and serve hot, with extra grated Parmesan, if liked.

Tagliatelle with Chicken

Spinach ribbon noodles covered with a rich tomato sauce and topped with creamy chicken makes this a very appetizing dish.

SERVES 4

Tomato Sauce (page 58)
250 g / 8 oz fresh green ribbon noodles
1 tbsp olive oil
salt
basil leaves, to garnish

Chicken sauce:
60 g / 2 oz / 4 tbsp unsalted butter
425 g / 14 oz boned, skinned chicken breast, thinly sliced
90 g / 3 oz / ½ cup blanched almonds
300 ml / ½ pint / 1¼ cups double (heavy) cream
salt and pepper

1 Make the tomato sauce, and keep warm.

2 To make the chicken sauce, melt the butter in a pan over a medium heat and fry the chicken strips and almonds for 5–6 minutes, stirring frequently, until the chicken is cooked through.

3 Meanwhile, pour the cream into a small pan over a low heat, bring it to the boil and boil for about 10 minutes, until reduced by almost half. Pour the cream over the chicken and almonds, stir well, and season. Set aside and keep warm.

4 Cook the pasta as described on page 59. Return the drained pasta to the saucepan, cover and keep warm.

5 Turn the pasta into a warmed serving dish and spoon over the tomato sauce. Spoon the chicken and cream over the centre, scatter the basil leaves and serve at once.

Aubergine (Eggplant) Cake

Layers of toasty-brown aubergine (eggplant), meat sauce and cheese-flavoured pasta.

SERVES 4

1 aubergine (eggplant), sliced thinly • 5 tbsp olive oil
250 g/ 8 oz short pasta shapes, such as fusilli
60 g/ 2 oz/ 4 tbsp butter, plus extra for greasing
45 g/ 1½ oz/ ⅓ cup flour • 300 ml/ ½ pint/ 1¼ cups milk
150 ml/ ¼ pint/ ⅔ cup single (light) cream
150 ml/ ¼ pint/ ⅔ cup chicken stock
large pinch of freshly grated nutmeg
90 g/ 3 oz/ 1¼ cups mature (sharp) Cheddar, grated
Lamb Sauce (page 59) • 30 g/ 1 oz/ ½ cup Parmesan, grated
salt and pepper • artichoke heart and tomato salad, to serve

1 Put the aubergine (eggplant) slices in a colander, sprinkle with salt and leave for 45 minutes. Rinse under cold running water and dry with paper towels. Heat 4 tablespoons of the oil in a pan over a medium heat. Fry the aubergine (eggplant) slices for about 4 minutes on each side, until golden. Remove with a slotted spoon and drain on paper towels.

2 Meanwhile, cook the pasta as described on page 59. Return the drained pasta to the pan. Cover and keep warm.

3 Melt the butter in a small pan, stir in the flour and cook for 1 minute. Gradually pour in the milk, stirring all the time, then stir in the cream and chicken stock. Season with nutmeg, salt and pepper, bring to the boil and simmer for 5 minutes. Stir in the Cheddar and remove the pan from the heat. Pour half the sauce over the pasta and mix well. Reserve the remaining sauce.

4 Grease a shallow ovenproof dish. Spoon in half the pasta, cover it with half the lamb sauce and then with the aubergines (eggplant)

in a single layer. Repeat the layers of pasta and lamb sauce and spread the remaining cheese sauce over the top of the final layer. Sprinkle with the Parmesan and bake in a preheated oven, 190°C/375°F/Gas Mark 5, for 25 minutes, until golden. Serve hot or cold, with artichoke heart and tomato salad.

Pasta with Green Vegetables

**The fresh vegetables make this a
mouthwateringly light summer dish.**

SERVES 4

250 g / 8 oz gemelli or other pasta shapes
1 tbsp olive oil
2 tbsp chopped fresh parsley
2 tbsp freshly grated Parmesan

Sauce:

1 head green broccoli, cut into florets
2 courgettes (zucchini), sliced
250 g / 8 oz asparagus spears, trimmed
125 g / 4 oz mangetout (snow peas), trimmed
125 g / 4 oz frozen peas • 30 g / 1 oz / 2 tbsp butter
3 tbsp vegetable stock • 5 tbsp double (heavy) cream
large pinch of freshly grated nutmeg • salt and pepper

1 Cook the pasta as described on page 59. Return the drained pasta to the saucepan, cover and keep warm.

2 To make the sauce, steam the broccoli, courgettes (zucchini), asparagus spears and mangetout (snow peas) over a pan of boiling, salted water until just beginning to soften. Remove from the heat and plunge into cold water to prevent further cooking. Drain and set aside. Cook the peas in boiling, salted water for 3 minutes, then drain. Refresh in cold water and drain again.

3 Put the butter and vegetable stock in a pan over a medium heat. Add all the vegetables except the asparagus spears and toss carefully with a wooden spoon, taking care not to break them up, until heated through. Stir in the cream, allow the sauce to just heat through and season well with salt, pepper and nutmeg.

4 Transfer the pasta to a warmed serving dish and stir in the chopped parsley. Spoon over the sauce, and sprinkle on the Parmesan. Arrange the asparagus spears on top. Serve hot.

Vegetarian Pasta & Bean Casserole

A satisfying winter one-pot meal.

SERVES 6

250 g/8 oz/dried haricot beans, soaked overnight and drained
250 g/8 oz penne, or other short pasta shapes
6 tbsp olive oil • 900 ml/1½ pints/3½ cups vegetable stock
2 large onions, sliced • 2 garlic cloves, chopped • 2 bay leaves
1 tsp dried oregano • 1 tsp dried thyme • 5 tbsp red wine
2 tbsp tomato purée (paste) • 2 celery stalks, sliced
1 fennel bulb, sliced • 125 g/4 oz mushrooms, sliced
250 g/8 oz tomatoes, sliced • 1 tsp dark muscovado sugar
4 tbsp dry white breadcrumbs • salt and pepper

To serve:
salad leaves • crusty bread

1 Put the beans in a large pan, cover with water and bring to the boil. Boil the beans rapidly for 20 minutes, then drain them.

2 Cook the pasta for only 3 minutes in a large pan of boiling salted water, adding 1 tablespoon of the oil. Drain in a colander and set aside.

3 Put the beans in a large flameproof casserole, pour over the vegetable stock and stir in the remaining olive oil, the onions, garlic, bay leaves, herbs, wine and tomato purée (paste). Bring to the boil, cover and cook in a preheated oven, 180°C/350°F/Gas Mark 4, for 2 hours.

4 Add the pasta, celery, fennel, mushrooms and tomatoes, and season. Stir in the sugar and sprinkle over the breadcrumbs. Cover the casserole and continue cooking for 1 hour. Serve hot, with salad leaves and plenty of crusty bread.

Vegetable Pasta Stir-Fry

**For an extra-quick dish, prepare all the
vegetables and cook the pasta in advance.**

SERVES 4

*425 g/14 oz wholewheat pasta shells,
or other short pasta shapes
1 tbsp olive oil • 2 carrots, sliced thinly
125 g/4 oz baby sweetcorn cobs • 3 tbsp peanut oil
2.5 cm/1 inch piece of ginger root, sliced thinly
1 large onion, sliced thinly • 1 garlic clove, sliced thinly
3 celery stalks, sliced thinly
1 small red (bell) pepper, cored, deseeded and
sliced into matchsticks
1 small green (bell) pepper, cored, deseeded and
sliced into matchsticks
salt • steamed mangetout (snow peas), to serve*

Sauce:
*1 tsp cornflour (cornstarch) • 2 tbsp water
3 tbsp soy sauce • 3 tbsp dry sherry
1 tsp clear honey • few drops of hot pepper sauce (optional)*

1 Cook the pasta as described on page 59. Return to the pan, cover and keep warm.

2 Boil the carrots and sweetcorn in salted water for 2 minutes. Drain, plunge into cold water to prevent further cooking and drain.

3 Heat the peanut oil in a wok or large frying pan (skillet) over a medium heat and fry the ginger for 1 minute, to flavour the oil. Remove the ginger with a slotted spoon and discard.

4 Add the onion, garlic, celery and (bell) peppers to the oil and stir-fry for 2 minutes. Add the carrots and sweetcorn, and stir-fry for 2 minutes, then stir in the reserved pasta.

5 To make the sauce, put the cornflour (cornstarch) into a small bowl with the water and mix to a smooth paste. Stir in the soy sauce, sherry and honey. Pour the sauce into the wok, stir well and cook for 2 minutes, stirring occasionally. Taste the sauce and season with hot pepper sauce, if liked. Serve with a steamed green vegetable such as mangetout (snow peas).

Baked Aubergines (Eggplant) with Pasta

Pasta, tomatoes and Mozzarella make a tasty filling for baked aubergine (eggplant).

SERVES 4

250 g/ 8 oz penne, or other short pasta shapes
4 tbsp olive oil, plus extra for brushing
2 aubergines (eggplant) • 1 large onion, chopped
2 garlic cloves, crushed
425 g/ 14 oz can of chopped tomatoes • 2 tsp dried oregano
60 g/ 2 oz Mozzarella, thinly sliced
30 g/ 1 oz/ ½ cup Parmesan, grated
2 tbsp dry breadcrumbs • salt and pepper
mixed salad leaves, to serve

1 Cook the pasta as described on page 59. Return to the pan, cover and keep warm.

2 Cut the aubergines (eggplant) in half lengthways. Score around the inside with a knife, then scoop out the flesh with a spoon, taking care not to pierce the skin. Brush the insides of the aubergine (eggplant) shells with olive oil. Chop the flesh and set it aside.

3 Heat the remaining oil in a frying pan (skillet) over a medium heat and fry the onion until it is translucent. Add the garlic and fry for 1 minute. Add the chopped aubergine (eggplant) and fry for 5 minutes, stirring frequently. Add the tomatoes and oregano, and season with salt and pepper. Bring to the boil and simmer for 10 minutes, or until the mixture is thick. Taste and adjust the seasoning if necessary. Remove from the heat and stir in the reserved pasta.

4 Brush a baking sheet (cookie sheet) with oil and arrange the aubergine (eggplant) shells in a single

layer. Divide half the tomato and pasta mixture between the four shells. Arrange the Mozzarella on top and cover with the remaining tomato and pasta mixture. Mix together the Parmesan and breadcrumbs, and sprinkle over the top, pressing it lightly into the mixture.

5 Bake in a preheated oven, 200°C/400°F/Gas Mark 6, for 25 minutes, until the topping is golden brown. Serve hot, with a mixed salad.

Béchamel Sauce

300 ml/½ pint/1¼ cups milk • 2 bay leaves
3 cloves • 1 small onion
60 g/2 oz/4 tbsp butter • 45 g/1½ oz/⅓ cup flour
300 ml/½ pint/1¼ cups single cream
large pinch of grated nutmeg
salt and pepper

1 Pour the milk into a small pan and add the bay leaves. Press the cloves into the onion, add to the pan and bring the milk to the boil. Remove the pan from the heat and set aside to cool.

2 Strain the milk into a jug and rinse the pan. Melt the butter in the pan, add the flour and stir for 1 minute. Gradually pour on the milk, stirring constantly. Cook the sauce for 3 minutes, then add the cream and bring to the boil. Remove from the heat and season with nutmeg, salt and pepper.

Tomato Sauce

2 tbsp olive oil • 1 small onion, chopped
1 garlic clove, chopped
1 × 424 g/14 oz can of chopped tomatoes
2 tbsp chopped parsley • 1 tsp dried oregano
2 bay leaves • 2 tbsp tomato purée (paste)
1 tsp sugar

1 Heat the oil in a pan over a medium heat and cook the onion until it is translucent. Add the garlic and cook for 1 minute.

2 Stir in the tomatoes, parsley, oregano, bay leaves, tomato purée (paste) and sugar and bring to the boil. Simmer, uncovered, for 15–20 minutes until the sauce has reduced by half. Taste and adjust the seasoning if necessary. Discard the bay leaves.

Lamb Sauce

2 tbsp olive oil
1 large onion, sliced
2 celery stalks, thinly sliced
500 g / 1 lb lean lamb, minced (ground)
3 tbsp tomato purée (paste)
150 g / 5 oz bottled sun-dried tomatoes, drained and chopped
1 tsp dried oregano
1 tbsp red wine vinegar
150 ml / ¼ pint / ⅔ cups chicken stock
salt and pepper

1 Heat the oil in a frying pan (skillet) over a medium heat. Add the onion and celery and cook until the onion is translucent. Add the lamb and cook, stirring frequently, until it browns.

2 Stir in the tomato purée (paste), sun-dried tomatoes, oregano, red wine vinegar and chicken stock, and season with salt and pepper to taste.

3 Bring the sauce to the boil and cook, uncovered, for about 20 minutes until the meat has absorbed the stock. Taste the sauce and adjust the seasoning if necessary.

Cooking Pasta

Cook pasta in a large pan of salted boiling water, to which you have added 1 tablespoon of olive oil; this will prevent the pieces of pasta from sticking together. When the pasta is almost tender, with a slight bite to it – the Italians describe it as *al dente* – remove from the heat and drain well in a colander.

Cooking times vary according to the type and volume of the pasta, and you should always follow those recommended on the packet. In general, fresh pasta cooks in 3–5 minutes, while dried pasta takes around 6 minutes.

Index